DREAM

BELIEVE

ACHIEVE

DATE:____/____/____

Thoughts have energy and when you read these quotes
that energy surrounds you and influence your
subconscious mind in a positive way. Work with these
quotes everyday by reading them and by writing your
thoughts and ideas in your inspirational journal –
notebook – diary.

Remember to always transform these words and quotes
into positive actions to start seeing the results you want.
Inspirational quotes are thoughts put into words, you
just need to add action and all your thoughts will
become a reality. Always Dream Big!

DATE:___/___/___

think positive

These inspirational quotes included in your motivational journal will boost your confidence and will remind you to take action. Once you read them every day, they will change your state of mind and you will start to feel more positive.

Every time you write on your journal – notebook – diary you will be reminded to move forward with a great positive and inspirational quote. Use these quotes as a part of your daily habits and routines by reading them and don't forget to write down your own thoughts and ideas in your new inspirational journal – notebook – diary.

"The best way to gain self-confidence is to do what you are afraid to do." – Unknown

DATE:___/___/___

MAKE IT HAPPEN

Remember to be consistent, be persistent and always be positive. These quotes will set your mind for success and achievement while you write down all your ideas and thoughts. You can share these quotes with your family and loved ones and gather to write down more great ideas and positive thoughts together. This beautiful inspirational journal – notebook – diary will bring you the support you need to move forward with a positive thinking mind. Let this journal be the tool for your daily inspiration.

To your success!

DATE:___/___/___

think positive

"Believe in miracles but above all believe in yourself!"

DATE:___/___/___

BELIEVE YOU CAN

DATE:____/____/____

think
positive

"Never downgrade your dreams, reach for the stars and
believe in your self power"

DATE:___/___/___

BELIEVE IN YOURSELF

DATE:___/___/___

think positive

"Never be afraid to start something new,
if you fail it is just temporary, if you believe and
persist you will succeed"

DATE:___/___/___

TAKE ACTION!

DATE:___/___/___

think
positive

"Wherever you go, go with all your heart." - Confucius

DATE:___/___/___

"Build your own dreams or you will end up building someone else's dreams"

never give up

DATE:___/___/___

think positive

"Your dreams and your goals are the seeds
of your own success"

DATE:___/___/___

MAKE IT
HAPPEN

DATE:___/___/___

think
positive

"Start where you are and take chances"

DATE:___/___/___

"If you never give up you become unbeatable,
just keep going!"

BELIEVE
YOU CAN

DATE: ___/___/___

think
positive

"Life isn't about finding yourself.
Life is about creating yourself." - George Bernard Shaw

DATE:___/___/___

BELIEVE IN YOURSELF

DATE:___/___/___

think positive

"CHANGE YOUR LIFE TODAY. DON'T GAMBLE ON THE FUTURE, ACT NOW, WITHOUT DELAY." — SIMONE DE BEAUVOIR

DATE:___/___/___

TAKE ACTION!

DATE: ___/___/___

think
positive

"AIM FOR THE STARS TO KEEP YOUR DREAMS ALIVE"

DATE:___/___/___

"There are no limits to what you can achieve if you believe in your dreams"

never
give
up

DATE:___/___/___

think
positive

"When you feel you are defeated, just remember,
you have the power to move on,
it is all in your mind"

DATE:___/___/___

MAKE IT HAPPEN

DATE:___/___/___

think positive

"OPPORTUNITY COMES TO THOSE WHO NEVER GIVE UP"

DATE:___/___/___

BELIEVE
YOU CAN

DATE:___/___/___

think
positive

"ALWAYS AIM FOR BIGGER GOALS, THEY HAVE
THE POWER TO KEEP YOU MOTIVATED"

DATE:___/___/___

BELIEVE IN
YOURSELF

DATE:___/___/___

think
positive

"SUCCESS IS NOT A PLACE OR A DESTINATION,
IT IS A WAY OF THINKING WHILE ALWAYS
HAVING A NEW GOAL IN MIND"

DATE:___/___/___

"Fall seven times and stand up eight." –
Japanese Proverb

TAKE ACTION!

DATE:___/___/___

think positive

"CHANGE THE WORLD ONE DREAM AT A TIME,
BELIEVE IN YOUR DREAMS"

DATE:___/___/___

"Dreams make things happen; nothing is impossible as long as you believe."

never
give
up

DATE:___/___/___

think positive

"Never loose confidence in your dreams,
there will be obstacles and defeats, but you will
always win if you persist"

DATE:___/___/___

MAKE IT
HAPPEN

DATE:___/___/___

think
positive

"Never wait for someone else to
validate your existence, you are the
creator of your own destiny"

DATE:___/___/___

BELIEVE
YOU CAN

DATE:___/___/___

think
positive

"Everything you dream is possible
as long as you believe in yourself"

DATE:___/___/___

BELIEVE IN YOURSELF

DATE:___/___/___

think positive

"A SUCCESSFUL PERSON IS SOMEONE THAT UNDERSTANDS TEMPORARY DEFEAT AS A LEARNING PROCESS, NEVER GIVE UP!"

DATE:___/___/___

TAKE ACTION!

DATE:___/___/___

think positive

"MOTIVATION COMES FROM WORKING ON OUR DREAMS AND
FROM TAKING ACTION TO ACHIEVE OUR GOALS"

DATE: ___/___/___

_____
_____
_____
_____
_____
_____
_____
_____
_____
_____
_____
_____
_____
_____
_____
_____
_____
_____
_____
_____
_____
_____
_____
_____
_____

DATE:___/___/___

think positive

"your mission in life should be to thrive
and not merely survive"

DATE:___/___/___

MAKE IT HAPPEN

DATE:___/___/___

think positive

"DOING WHAT YOU BELIEVE IN, AND GOING AFTER YOUR DREAMS WILL ONLY RESULT IN SUCCESS." - ANONYMOUS

DATE:____/____/____

BELIEVE YOU CAN

DATE:_____/_____/_____

think
positive

"The will to win, the desire to succeed, the urge to reach your full potential... these are the keys that will unlock the door to personal excellence." – Confucius

DATE:___/___/___

BELIEVE IN YOURSELF

DATE:___/___/___

think positive

"LET YOUR DREAMS BE BIGGER THAN YOUR FEARS AND YOUR ACTIONS
LOUDER THAN YOUR WORDS." - ANONYMOUS

DATE:___/___/___

TAKE
ACTION!

DATE:___/___/___

think positive

"START EVERY DAY WITH A GOAL IN MIND AND
MAKE IT HAPPEN WITH YOUR ACTIONS"

DATE:___/___/___

DATE:___/___/___

think
positive

"If you have big dreams you will always
have big reasons to wake up every day"

"To achieve our dreams we must
first overcome our fear of failure"

MAKE IT
HAPPEN

DATE:___/___/___

think
positive

"Difficulties are nothing more than
Opportunities in disguise, keep On
trying and you will succeed"

DATE:___/___/___

BELIEVE YOU CAN

DATE:___/___/___

think positive

"Always have a powerful reason to wake up
every new morning, set goals and follow your dreams"

DATE:___/___/___

BELIEVE IN YOURSELF

DATE:___/___/___

think positive

"NEVER LET YOUR DREAMS DIE FOR FEAR OF FAILURE.
DEFEAT IS JUST TEMPORARY: YOUR DREAMS ARE YOUR POWER"

DATE:___/___/___

TAKE
ACTION!

DATE:___/___/___

think positive

"A FAILURE IS A LESSON, NOT A LOSS. IT IS A TEMPORARY
AND SOMETIMES NECESSARY DETOUR, NOT A DEAD END"

DATE:___/___/___

never give up

DATE:___/___/___

"Never let your doubt blind your goals, for your future lies in your ability, not your failure" — *Anonymous*

"Don't go into something to test the waters, go into things to make waves"
— *Anonymous*

MAKE IT HAPPEN

DATE:___/___/___

think positive

"Laughter is the shock absorber that softens and minimizes the bumps of life" — Anonymous

DATE:___/___/___

"Dream – Believe – Achieve"

BELIEVE YOU CAN

DATE:___/___/___

think
positive

"HOPE IS A WAKING DREAM" - ARISTOTLE

DATE:___/___/___

BELIEVE IN YOURSELF

DATE:___/___/___

think positive

"NEVER GIVE UP ON A DREAM JUST BECAUSE OF THE TIME IT WILL TAKE
TO ACCOMPLISH IT. THE TIME WILL PASS ANYWAY."
– ANONYMOUS

DATE:___/___/___

TAKE
ACTION!

DATE:___/___/___

think
positive

"IF YOU WANT TO FEEL RICH, JUST COUNT ALL THE THINGS
YOU HAVE THAT MONEY CAN'T BUY" — ANONYMOUS

DATE:___/___/___

never give up

DATE:___/___/___

think positive

"Some pursue success and
happiness – others create it"
— Anonymous

DATE:___/___/___

MAKE IT
HAPPEN

think
positive

"IT'S BETTER TO HAVE AN IMPOSSIBLE DREAM THAN
NO DREAM AT ALL" — ANONYMOUS

DATE:____/____/____

BELIEVE YOU CAN

DATE:___/___/___

think
positive

"The winner always has a plan; The loser always
has an excuse" — Anonymous

DATE:___/___/___

BELIEVE IN YOURSELF

DATE:___/___/___

think
positive

"There is no elevator to success.
you have to take the stairs"
— Anonymous

DATE: ___/___/___

"Never let defeat have the last word" — Anonymous

DATE:___/___/___

think positive

"DON'T LET YESTERDAY'S DISAPPOINTMENTS, OVERSHADOW
TOMORROW'S ACHIEVEMENTS" — ANONYMOUS

DATE:____/____/____

"Hope is a waking dream." –
Aristotle

DATE:___/___/___

think
positive

"WE ARE LIMITED, NOT BY OUR ABILITIES, BUT BY OUR VISION"
— ANONYMOUS

DATE:___/___/___

"The mind is everything. What you think you become." – Buddha

MAKE IT HAPPEN

DATE: ___/___/___

think positive

"A JOURNEY OF A THOUSAND MILES MUST BEGIN
WITH A SINGLE STEP." – LAO TZU

DATE:___/___/___

BELIEVE YOU CAN

DATE:___/___/___

think
positive

"A diamond is a chunk of coal that
made good under pressure"
— Anonymous

DATE:___/___/___

BELIEVE IN
YOURSELF

DATE:___/___/___

think positive

"REMEMBER YESTERDAY, DREAM OF TOMORROW, BUT LIVE FOR TODAY" — ANONYMOUS

DATE:___/___/___

TAKE ACTION!

DATE:___/___/___

think
positive

"Dream is not what you see in sleep, dream is the thing
which does not let you sleep" — Anonymous

DATE:___/___/___

never
give
up

DATE:___/___/___

think
positive

"DON'T BE PUSHED BY YOUR PROBLEMS.
BE LED BY YOUR DREAMS" — ANONYMOUS

DATE:___/___/___

MAKE IT HAPPEN

DATE:___/___/___

think
positive

"ONCE YOU HAVE A DREAM PUT ALL YOUR HEART
AND SOUL TO ACHIEVE IT"

DATE:___/___/___

BELIEVE YOU CAN

DATE:___/___/___

think
positive

"YOU CREATE YOUR LIFE BY FOLLOWING
YOUR DREAMS WITH DECISIVE ACTIONS"

DATE:___/___/___

BELIEVE IN
YOURSELF

DATE:___/___/___

think positive

"The road to success is always full of surprises
and temporary failures, real success comes
to those who persist and enjoy the journey"

DATE:___/___/___

TAKE ACTION!

DATE:___/___/___

think
positive

"TO live a creative life, we must lose
our fear of being wrong"
- Anonymous

DATE:___/___/___

"Believe and act as if it were
impossible to fail."

never
give
up

DATE:___/___/___

think positive

"MAKE EACH DAY COUNT, YOU WILL NEVER
HAVE THIS DAY AGAIN"

"It's not what you look at that matters,
it's what you see" - Anonymous

MAKE IT HAPPEN

DATE:___/___/___

think
positive

"SUCCESSFUL PEOPLE MAKE A HABIT OF DOING WHAT
UNSUCCESSFUL PEOPLE DON'T WANT TO DO"
— ANONYMOUS

DATE:___/___/___

BELIEVE
YOU CAN

DATE:___/___/___

think positive

Be Strong! It might be stormy
now, but it can't rain forever!"
- Anonymous

DATE:___/___/___

BELIEVE IN YOURSELF

DATE:___/___/___

BELIEVE IN YOURSELF

"Be Strong! It might be stormy now,
but it can't rain forever!" - Anonymous
"

DATE:___/___/___

BELIEVE IN YOURSELF

DATE:___/___/___

BELIEVE IN YOURSELF

DATE:___/___/___

"It doesn't matter what you look like on the outside. It's what's on the inside that counts"
- Unknown

BELIEVE IN YOURSELF

DATE:____/____/____

BELIEVE IN YOURSELF

DATE:___/___/___

"Stop hating yourself for everything you aren't. Start loving yourself for everything that you are" - Unknown

BELIEVE IN YOURSELF

DATE:___/___/___

BELIEVE IN YOURSELF

DATE:___/___/___

BELIEVE IN YOURSELF

DATE:___/___/___

"Don't let a bad day make you feel like
you have a bad life" – Unknown